Dear Dad

S. S. Nightshade

It took me a while to publish this. I can't even really explain what this is. A release? A prayer? Another random shout into the ever–expanding void?

Despite the title, this isn't for him. It's not a cry for him to come back, to apologize or to change. And it's not a cry for attention.

It's me ripping the god damn duct tape off my mouth about it. It's me acknowledging it, instead of burying it underneath my anger and hurt to keep everyone else around me comfortable.

This is what it was, simply, painfully.

When I knew him, he was an abusive, neglectful narcissist. But he also had a gentle soul. A respect for our world. Getting to a point where you can empathize with the people who hurt you is an experience words can't describe. But I tried.

There is no trigger warning I can give you. These are my blurry emotions and memories. I just needed to get them out.

-Nightshade

How I Worry

I worry about the day you die

Will I even know when it happens?

Will your new family call me

expecting me to handle your body

or wanting me to be present?

Will I have no idea until months

or *years* later?

I worry you love them more than you ever loved me

I worry they know a version of you I never met

I worry that they love you so much

that they can't understand my anger.

I worry that like me

you worry you'll never see me again

I worry that you'll die sad because of it

I worry that I won't forgive myself for it

This is how I worry now.

The Mirror

My eyes are blue.

Not brown like my mothers,

and not bright icicles like hers...

They're deep,

moving,

river water.

Murky and green,

with specks of glittering gold kissing my iris,

and sun–dried dirt.

Hazel...

dulling,

bleaching,

no longer saturated.

I used to love

my color changing eyes...

Now it's your eyes which stare back at me,

the ashes of our burned bridge...

My eyes were blue.

You know my name

this one

the mask…

Nightshade.

Poisonous, yet beautiful.

Dark, yet blooming.

You know this is me

because you told me that I could be this,

that you would accept any version of me

that I called myself.

I sometimes get my hopes up

wondering if you know

wondering if you get your hands on anything–

everything

that I wrote

write…

I wonder if my books are added to your pile

I wonder if they'll be burned when you're gone

The Drive

That was where we broke

I felt it happen, even as you said nothing

Even as you said everything

That car ride to the hospital

The most vulnerable

The most intimate

You didn't say anything to hurt me

I barely remember a word

But I remember the words didn't hurt

The atmosphere did

I could feel you detaching

Spiraling

Leaving me

Long before you actually didn't come home

I felt when you stopped hanging on

To trying to love me

When I finally became too much for you

I still love the woods

The forests

The farms

The creek beds

The deer paths

The loud ass squirrels

The crows…

I will never escape you there

I will never be alone there

Because you're breathing down my neck

Your voice penetrating my memory

Pointing out the prints

The track

The way….

I feel your smile on my skin as I sprint through the trees

The corn

The dark

After

Mom was not okay after you left

The tether on her paranoia snapped

Stress was her only meal for three years

Anger was her only rest

And panic kept her going

That I would die

That you would take me

That I would also want to leave her

She might have been damaged, but you knew that

You chose that

And instead of nurturing it

You were neglectful

Instead of being gentle

You were not

And then you left her

For me to fix

For me to love

For me

My Marriage

I see you in myself

When I'm fighting with my husband

Your fist is going through my wall

Your foot is sending my furniture across the room

Your voice is bellowing out of my chest

Carving me open

I would rather die than abuse my husband

As you abused us

But here I am breathing in my next breath

To yell again

Where You Went

For a while I wanted you back

Like a toxic ex

I'm the one who told you to leave, I know

So I shouldn't have been whining

"My Daddy left me!"

But I was sixteen

And you were in your fifties

You listened to an angry teenager

A scared teenager

Who was begging her parents to stop fighting

And before that

You were gone for months at a clip anyway

You ended your marriage, fine

But you left your child

And then blamed her for it

An Accusation

You stopped touching me

Because I would fight back

Your boot hit my spine when I was three

My bat hit yours when I was ten

You flipped my mattress over with me on it

I kicked out your chair to send you sprawling

Your fist went through a wall that I had dented

Your knife went through a window past my head

Your foot kicked my old dog in the gut

And I told you I would kill you

You were getting older

I was getting stronger

And angrier

A Can of Tuna Fish

You fed me roadkill

And vegetables from our garden

You didn't even open a can of tuna fish

For your wife

For a month

She bashed it open with a rock

To not starve

Competition

You already lost because I was a girl

My only cousin was a boy

So I was automatically weaker

Slower

Dumber

Softer

Less…

No matter how athletic I was

He was a boy

No matter how intelligent

He was a boy

No matter how special

He. Was. A. Boy.

In a legacy of male heirs

I was a girl

So you already lost

Before I failed you

Poor 1

You got what you wanted

And live in denial

When you left us for Her

I would have been charged

All your debt

If mom didn't pay it back

You skipped child support just shy of illegal

And avoided college like the plague

Forget about starting out money

Because you were finished with me

After your abuse, and neglect

You were handed your dream life on a golden platter

A house in the mountains

On a lake

With acreage

And you don't need to work much anymore

Meanwhile

I'll work till I'm dead

Poor 2

We never had money for everything

We had to pick and choose

Heat

Hot water

Electric

Or food

Two was asking for a lot

Three was next to impossible

All four were for the rich people

But

We still built a hunting hut in the backyard

For you

But we forgot to buy me books for school

The Farm 1

It was the only place I ever saw you happy

Finding abandoned shotgun shells

Letting me and the dogs run loose

Sledding down the hill

Or sweating in the fields

Or walking through the woods

All year

Only seeing Mr. Tightlips, The Gobbler,

Out of season when you couldn't shoot

And the dumb brother bucks

Somehow surviving each year together

I have that place memorized

Like the back of my hand

If I just shut my eyes

I can smell it

The Farm 2

There's a Christmas Tree graveyard

At the back of the property

Up the drive

Past the corn field

And over the hill

There must be over ten trees there

I used to think there were hundreds

I was so little

It was so big to me

But no more than fourteen, now that I'm counting

The years

It's morbid to think

That there's a grave of happy memories

Given back to nature

That the cycle went on

Without me

I only ever shot a gun once

I was too little for the kick

But you had me practice it anyway

It hurt my ears

And left bruises

I prefer archery

The finesse

The silence

Like an assassin, waiting in the trees

You still have my bow

I won't let you use it as a bribe anymore

I'll buy a new one

And start over

The Blood of Christ

I think it's fitting

that with your blood pressure

you can't drink, like the rest of us

To forget

To feel better

You get no relief

No oblivion

The only thing that's good for your heart

is the wine

The only thing you can partake in

is attempting to cleanse yourself—

absolve yourself

of the sins you deny committing

Apologies

There are things I feel bad for

Looking back as an adult

That I know hurt you

And my naïve child brain didn't realize it

But mom did

The jokes, were actually mocking

The anger, was two sided

Many things shouldn't have been said

Or done

But I can't be the bigger person

My inner child is far too hurt

To say sorry to a Father

Who denies it happened

Why I'm Gone

You pushed me

I could understand you leaving, after a time

But you pushed me afterwards

Boundaries were not allowed

Comfort zones didn't matter

The years of absence, of sadness

Weren't acknowledged

And you didn't really change

You were happier

But that man I remembered

Still surfaced when I was around

I don't know why I expected

The over sexual, uncomfortable, misogynistic, gross

Things to stop

I don't know why I expected

Respect

Or help

I don't know why I expected

My feelings to be validated

For you to admit that you fucked up

But you pretended things didn't happen

You pretended you didn't yell

Hit

Intimidate

Leave

You victimized yourself

You made yourself a martyr

You were too busy

Moving on

To see I was still black and blue

From the previous version of you

The version of you who would hurt my family

If I didn't give you what you want

And now you have what you want anyway

And it isn't me

So this time

I left you

Her

I really hate

that I like you

I don't blame you

and I'm not mad at you

for loving my father

you didn't take him from me

he left me all on his own

and you should take his side

you love him

that's okay

but please don't come into my life later

when he's gone

with opinions or feelings

about how I can't

because you weren't there to see him with us

He's better with you

so much better

and that's enough

I regularly want to call you

To fix this

To save us

I want you in my life so damn bad

That sometimes

my ribs feel like they're serrating me

from the inside out

I need to remind myself what you did to me

to stay away

I need to remind myself what you did to ME

not mom

to stay away

I need to remind myself you never apologized

I need to remind myself that every time I found you

it hurt worse than missing you

Estranged

It was the first big word I learned

The descriptor

adults would use

to describe my relationship with you

When you left

When I didn't know if you were alive or dead

When I didn't know if I would ever see you again

When you showed up at my high school graduation

and everyone saw you

When you showed up at my college one

and no one saw you

Stranger

Mom didn't even know what you looked like

when she saw you for the last time

You were on vacation

close enough to a game I was playing

to come watch me

She saw you, smiled, walked past

You gaped at her

went white as a sheet

She remembered the look on "that man's face"

and hoped he was okay

because she didn't understand your look

because she didn't know it was you

You really are unrecognizable now

your hair long

your eyes bright

I broke down on the bus

grateful you didn't hurt her again

The Hospital Questionnaire

They really wanted to take me away

because I didn't keep my mouth shut

because I told them

About when you threw that knife at me

how it passed my face, and shattered the window

because I struggled with my homework

About our matching holes in the wall

my fist learning by watching yours

About boiling water during the winter

so I could bathe without freezing

About only getting new food once a month

and watching my mom not eat so that I could

About the roadkill in the freezer

About the ghosts

About the bullies

Once I started telling them I couldn't stop

and then I had to lie

to go home

It Will End With Me

I don't remember exactly what I told my Gods

but I told them that this torture

this abuse, neglect, and anger

would end with me

I will be the last

that may mean I will never have children

at least, not give birth

I want to once, twice maybe

I have the names picked out

But I have a body that I'm worried can't bear it

There will always be children in my life

whether flesh and blood or not

Regardless…

I'm breaking the halo, forming the horns

I'll go to hell for it, surely

but this cycle ends with me

The Ball

I'm sewing a gown

Stripping the fabric off an old one you never saw

And stitching by hand

A new one, you'll never see

You taught me how to sew

If it looks horrible

It's your fault

If it looks lovely

It's because of you

So you'll be with me, there

Embedded in the thread

For the father daughter dance

We never had

You never concerned yourself

With the minor details

When it came to my comfort or safety

I ripped my eyebrow open on a rusty nail

You poured alcohol into it

Because I was already screaming anyway

I had a tick on my face

Seconds before it bit

You had the sharpened blade of an arrow slicing me

To get it off

Because that was in your hand already

There was a mountain lion at the farm one day

Within three hundred yards

I was little

The perfect size for prey

But you wanted to follow it anyway

Fishing

Mom caught that fish

The one you stole

From your trip to Canada

Mounted in your new bedroom

I sometimes think

You always wanted to take me fishing there

So you could actually catch one yourself

I've never gone fishing without you

We were supposed to

The last day we spoke

When I thought you found out where I lived

And cut you off again

Church

I tried to be a good Christian American Girl

But when I was abandoned

By you and the church

Simply for hurting a little too much

It wasn't Jesus that saved me

It wasn't modesty that protected me

It wasn't repentance that raised me out of that hell

The moon

The hounds

The foxes

The ravens

The dark

They are who saved me

And sometimes they're terrifying

But sometimes, so am I

I still pray every night

I'm still an acolyte at an alter

Just not yours

For years after you left

I couldn't stand the scent of oranges

I would gag

I would retch

I would be plagued by the memory

Of you carving off the peel with one of your pocketknives

Balancing on the edge of your Chicago Bears trash can

Always eating it a few feet away

Despite me saying I didn't like the smell

A decade later

A bottle from the apothecary

It was that poignant smell

It was that overbearing scent

I endured it

Remembering you

As I learned to take care of myself

Lilac's

Our yard is destroyed

The rose bushes torn out

The honeysuckle ripped down

The morning glories weed wacked

The pumpkin patch overgrown

The azaleas cut down

The vegetable boxes thrown away

The evergreen bushes removed

The lilac bush

Gone

Gram

I'm quite a lot like your mother

Emotions a hurricane

Interests various

Chaos in human form

I'm growing my own rock garden

With crystals she would love

I'm excellent at word puzzles

The ones she taught me how

I feel her in my chest

Her joy is palpable

Our spirits chattering across the veil

And every day I get dressed

Choosing from the wild prints in my closet

Or donning my eyes with purple glitter

We laugh

Storage

The only time I saw you as an older teenager

was to help you clean our lives out

of the storage unit

You needed an extra pair of hands

there was so much

from the house

So much that wasn't yours

So much I couldn't take

But I got some

I took your families glass decanter

the cookbook with Grammys notes

Gram's silver mirror

and boxes and boxes and boxes

of photographs

the proof that once

we were happy

Plants

I still don't know the name of it

Grammy's plant

The spikey green one

That occasionally bloomed

A tall,

Dangling,

White flower

I don't have the original

That's long dead

In a place I don't know

But I have one

A small one

A mimic

Keeping the tradition alive

Fathers

We both wound up not having a dad

Yours died

A car

A telephone pole

A widow with three young boys

Mine left

A car

A woman

A mother with a suicidal child

You knew the pain of not having a Father

So how could

you leave

me

Dusk

One of my favorite things to do

still

is crawl the car around the countryside

right before the night sets in

looking for the deer

counting the points on a buck

trying to find the rare

black or white one

maybe a piebald

I don't do it often

but there's times I get home late from work

because I was trying to find the deer

like we used to

Education

I learned far more than you gave me credit for

I paid attention

I worshipped

The way you worked with the Earth

The tracking

The patience

The kill

The give and take

The careful draw of a blade against the hide

The shape of berries

The textures of plants

The durability of stone

The wet and dry of leaves and kindling

The curved alcove against the wind

That you need to survive

If I'm lost in the woods

I'll live

Call Me Crazy

I'm writing to a man I want out of my life

I'm having hopes that he still wants me

As desperately as I want him

He didn't beat me

But he did hit

He didn't starve me

But I was hungry

I don't feel like I was neglected

But I didn't have basic necessities

The reasons I need to stay away are clear

Understandable

Fair

But he left me

      He left me

            He left me

Before I was old enough to make the choice

Easter

I was sixteen years old

the first time I called the cops

because after being missing for three months

you burst in

screaming for your gun

that you had to sell it

that you were in trouble

Mom told me to run

the dogs and I

took off along the riverbank

the sun beating down

nowhere to hide

I was very calm on the phone

so that they didn't shoot you

even though I didn't know

if you wanted to shoot her

I grew up in a pack

with an Alpha Mother

with the hounds on the hunt

with the Father, the Master

I know the functions

how to bare my teeth

how to show submission

and I think that's why I have cats now

I am a lone wolf

and I am tired

and they let me nap

they give me space

There is no hierarchy

just being

Love

I became a runner for years

because I watched you leave

because I watched mom follow

until you disappeared

I was taught to run

toward the hurt

toward the danger

toward the promise of being gutted

I was taught to expect it

I was not taught how to handle Him

My love

My dearest

My eye in the storm

I am the storm

And when I ran

he would not chase me, instead

A slow, steady walk

to not spook me

A soft, gentle voice

to settle my nerves

He basked in my storm

as I tried to drown him

I ran more than once

fleeing from his sunlight

like the darkness which I am

You taught me how to run

not love

that I taught myself

which is how I know you never felt it

for me

Insomnia

You thought to tire me out

Sit-ups at midnight

Stand on one leg

Balance the cold gallon of milk over your head

Until you're sleepy enough to spill it

And get your ass in bed

I'm sleeping soundly for the first time in my life

It took four years of lying beside Him

To forget the stress of going to sleep

Yours

I often find myself angry

Aware

It took a long time to make myself into a wolf

To sharpen my teeth

To become the monster

To protect myself

Against those who hurt me

And I can

I do

I snap my teeth

I howl in rage

In mourning

In promise

But you

You I cannot hunt

Because I am your fawn

And always will be

Grave

If I know

I will find you

I will say a proper goodbye

And when I too am nothing left but ash

Maybe we can try once more

www.ingramcontent.com/pod-product-compliance
Lightning Source LLC
Chambersburg PA
CBHW031244130726
47988CB00008B/3237